RHYTHMS OF COMPASSION

A POETIC JOURNEY THROUGH ANI CHOYING DROLMA'S LIFE AND LEGACY

TANVITH REDDY

This book is dedicated to **Amish Tripathi**, a visionary storyteller who has inspired me to delve into the world of myth, religion, and spirituality. Your works have kindled our imagination and made us see the world with new eyes.

Contents

Foreword

Foreword

It is my great pleasure to write this foreword for this book, a poetic tribute to the life and legacy of Ani Choying Drolma, a revered Buddhist nun, singer, and activist. This book is a celebration of Ani Choying's inspiring journey and the positive impact she has made on the world through her music and activism.

Ani Choying's story is one of remarkable resilience and compassion. Her early life was marked by hardship and adversity, yet she never lost her sense of purpose or her commitment to her faith. Through her music, she has touched the hearts of countless people, inspiring them to embrace their own spiritual traditions and to work towards a more compassionate world.

In this book, the author takes us on a journey through Ani Choying's life, from her childhood to her rise to fame as a performer and recording artist, and on to her philanthropic work and lasting legacy. Through the power of verse, the author brings Ani Choying's story to life, showcasing her remarkable spirit and the profound impact she has had on those around her.

As we journey through the pages of this book, I hope that readers will be inspired by Ani Choying's life and the power of her music and activism. I believe that her story has the potential to touch the hearts of people from all walks of life, and to inspire them to make a positive impact on the world.

I am honored to introduce this book and to share in the celebration of Ani Choying Drolma's life and legacy. I hope that it will inspire readers to embrace their own spirituality, to work towards a more compassionate world, and to make a positive impact on the lives of those around them.

Prologue

In a land of mountains high and rivers wide, A voice did rise, both gentle and strong. A voice that sang of love and peace, And of the path that leads to right.

A voice that spoke of wisdom old, Of compassion's might, and spirit's flight. A voice that carried with it hope, And of the power of the human heart.

And as the singer journeyed forth, She brought to life the stories untold. She sang of joy and sang of pain, And of the endless journey of the soul.

With every note, she touched a heart, And inspired countless to follow her lead. To seek the path of love and peace, And to make a world that's kinder indeed.

And so we journey with her now, Along the road of song and faith. And we tell her story, verse by verse, So that her message lives on in grace.

I. Introduction

An angelic voice that fills the air,
Ani Choying Drolma, her name is rare.
From the land of Nepal, she brings her grace,
Her music and kindness, a shining space.
Born in the hills of Nepal, in a nunnery fair,
Ani Choying's story, a journey to share.
Raised in the Buddhist faith, her spirit took flight,
Her voice, a gift, her passion, to bring light.
She trained in classical Tibetan music, from an early age,
Her voice, a talent, a powerful stage.
Her music, a blend of tradition and modern appeal,
Her spirit and her songs, a beautiful seal.
With each note she sings, her voice rings true,
Ani Choying's life, a story to imbue.
Her music and her mission, a source of inspiration,
A nun, a singer, a philanthropist with a pure heart's foundation.
A singer, a nun, a philanthropist too,
Ani Choying's life, a tale to imbue.
Her music transcends, and touches the soul,
Her heart, a source of kindness, making her whole.
She sings of love and compassion, day by day,
Her voice, a ray of hope, leading the way.
Her work for the less fortunate, a noble cause,
Ani Choying Drolma, a shining star, applause!

II. Early Life

Ani Choying Drolma, born in the hills so steep,
In a nunnery, her childhood was complete.
Her family, steeped in the Buddhist faith,
Her spirit and love, a beautiful grace.
Her parents, devout, with hearts full of care,
Their love, a guiding light, always there.
Ani Choying's childhood, a tale to unfold,
Her spirit and love, a story untold.
She grew up surrounded by love and peace,
Her parents and community, her source of release.
Her childhood, filled with laughter and song,
Her spirit and love, always strong.
The hills of Nepal, her home, so serene,
Ani Choying's childhood, a life serene.
Her family, a source of love and support,
Her spirit and passion, a guiding resort.
Ani Choying's spirit, a light in the dark,
Her faith and her music, a beautiful spark.
Her introduction to Buddhism, at a young age,
Her spirit and love, a powerful sage.
The teachings of the Buddha, a source of peace,
Her heart and her spirit, a release.
Her introduction to music, a gift from above,
Her voice and her spirit, filled with love.
She learned the ways of the faith, with a pure heart,
Her spirit and love, a beautiful art.
Her introduction to music, a journey to unfold,
Her voice and her spirit, a tale untold.

Her heart and her voice, a perfect harmony,
Ani Choying's life, a beautiful symphony.
She learned the ways of the faith, with grace,
Her spirit and her music, a beautiful place.
Ani Choying's training, in the ways of the faith,
Her spirit and her love, a source of grace.
She learned the ways of classical Tibetan music, with care,
Her voice and her spirit, a tale to share.
Her education, a journey of growth and light,
Her spirit and her voice, a source of delight.
She trained with the masters, of the Tibetan art,
Her voice and her spirit, a beautiful heart.
Her voice and her spirit, a perfect match,
Her training and education, a journey to catch.
Ani Choying's life, a testament to love,
Her heart and her voice, a symbol from above.
Her training and education, a source of pride,
Her spirit and her voice, a journey worldwide.
She learned the ways of the faith, with devotion,
Her voice and her spirit, a beautiful emotion.

III. Rise to Fame

Ani Choying's voice, a source of delight,
Her performances, a journey to ignite.
Her early shows, a source of inspiration,
Her voice and her spirit, a beautiful sensation.
She sang of love and compassion, with grace,
Her voice and her spirit, a beautiful place.
Her early recordings, a source of delight,
Her voice and her spirit, shining bright.
Her music, a blend of tradition and modern appeal,
Her voice and her spirit, a source of appeal.
Her early performances, a journey to unfold,
Her voice and her spirit, a tale untold.
Ani Choying's voice, a source of unity,
Her collaborations, a source of diversity.
She worked with other musicians, from near and far,
Her voice and her spirit, shining like a star.
Her collaborations, a source of inspiration,
Her voice and her spirit, a beautiful sensation.
She brought together different cultures and sounds,
Her voice and her spirit, a beautiful harmony found.
Her music, a source of love and peace,
Her collaborations, a journey to release.
She brought together different styles and traditions,
Her voice and her spirit, a beautiful fusion.
Ani Choying's voice, a source of peace,
Her tours and concerts, a journey to release.
She traveled the world, spreading her love,
Her voice and her spirit, shining from above.

Her concerts, a source of inspiration,
Her voice and her spirit, a beautiful sensation.
She sang of love and compassion, with grace,
Her voice and her spirit, a beautiful place.
Her tours and concerts, a journey worldwide,
Her voice and her spirit, shining bright.
She brought her message of love and peace,
Her voice and her spirit, a source of release.
Her music, a source of hope and light,
Her tours and concerts, a journey in sight.
Ani Choying's life, a beautiful tale,
Her voice and her spirit, shining like a sail.

IV. Philanthropic Work

Ani Choying, a voice of compassion,
Her philanthropic work, a beautiful action.
She founded the Nuns Welfare Foundation,
Her spirit and her mission, a beautiful sensation.
Her mission, to empower and support,
The nuns of Nepal, to uplift and comfort.
She founded this organization, with love,
Her spirit and her mission, a source of hope from above.
Her foundation, a source of education and health,
For the nuns of Nepal, to uplift and strengthen their wealth.
She provided a safe and nurturing place,
Her spirit and her mission, a source of grace.
Her foundation, a source of support and care,
For the nuns of Nepal, to uplift and repair.
Ani Choying's philanthropic work, a beautiful tale,
Her spirit and her mission, shining like a sail.
Ani Choying's voice, a source of kindness,
Her charitable initiatives, a source of love, so divine.
She worked to improve the lives of those in need,
Her spirit and her mission, a source of good deed.
Her initiatives, a source of hope and light,
For those in need, to uplift and unite.
She provided food, shelter, and clothing, with care,
Her spirit and her mission, a source of repair.
She worked with the marginalized and the poor,
Her spirit and her mission, a source of love, to restore.
She provided education and skills to those in need,
Her spirit and her mission, a source of love, indeed.

Her charitable initiatives, a source of love, so pure,
For those in need, to uplift and endure.
Ani Choying's philanthropic work, a beautiful tale,
Her spirit and her mission, shining like a sail.
C. Impact on communities in Nepal
Ani Choying's voice, a source of change,
Her impact on communities, a beautiful exchange.
She worked to improve the lives of those in need,
Her spirit and her mission, a source of good deed.
Her work, a source of hope and progress,
For communities in Nepal, to uplift and redress.
She provided education and healthcare, with love,
Her spirit and her mission, a source of hope from above.
She worked to empower women and girls, with grace,
Her spirit and her mission, a beautiful place.
She provided skills and opportunities, with care,
Her spirit and her mission, a source of repair.
Her impact on communities, a source of change,
For those in need, to uplift and arrange.
Ani Choying's philanthropic work, a beautiful tale,
Her spirit and her mission, shining like a sail.

V. Legacy and Contribution

Ani Choying, a voice of inspiration,
Her music, a source of Buddhist meditation.
Her voice and her music, a source of peace,
Her legacy, a source of love, never to cease.
Her music, a source of love and harmony,
Influencing modern Buddhist music, so heavenly.
Her voice, a source of beauty, so serene,
Her music, a source of enlightenment, a scene.
Her music, a source of spiritual connection,
Influencing modern Buddhist music, a reflection.
Her voice, a source of compassion and love,
Her music, a source of hope from above.
Her influence on modern Buddhist music, so great,
Her voice and her music, a source of spiritual state.
Ani Choying's legacy, a source of inspiration,
Her music, a source of love and meditation.
Ani Choying, a voice of love and change,
Her music and activism, a source of beautiful range.
Her voice, a source of peace, so divine,
Her activism, a source of hope and change, align.
Her music, a source of spiritual connection,
Her activism, a source of hope and reflection.
Her voice and her music, a source of love,
Her activism, a source of hope from above.
Her activism, a source of change, so real,
Her voice and her music, a source of love, so ideal.
Her activism, a source of empowerment and care,
Her voice and her music, a source of hope, to repair.

Her significance, a source of hope and change,
Her music and activism, a beautiful exchange.
Ani Choying's legacy, a source of inspiration,
Her music and activism, a source of love and liberation.
Ani Choying, a voice of love and hope,
Her legacy, a source of inspiration, to cope.
Her voice and her music, a source of peace,
Her legacy, a source of love, to never cease.
Her legacy, a source of inspiration and love,
For future generations, to uplift and improve.
Her voice and her music, a source of hope and light,
Her legacy, a source of change, so bright.
Her legacy, a source of empowerment and care,
For future generations, to uplift and repair.
Her voice and her music, a source of spiritual connection,
Her legacy, a source of love, for future generations.
Her legacy, a source of hope and change,
For future generations, to uplift and arrange.
Ani Choying's legacy, a source of inspiration,
Her music and activism, a source of love and liberation.

www.ingramcontent.com/pod-product-compliance
Lightning Source LLC
Chambersburg PA
CBHW022048150726
47990CB00004B/1650